Plot Wizard™ Flash Fiction

A "Genie" to Create Original Content Structure in Minutes for Short Stories

derived from works

by **Wycliffe A. Hill**

and based on the
"Plot Genie Supplemental Formula No. 6 "Short-Short Story"

"Plot Wizard" is a trademark owned by Midwest Journal Press.

Table of Contents

EDITOR NOTES:

References to the use of a "Wizard" or "Genie" are for a random number generator that produces a result between 1 and 180. Many online versions are available. A spreadsheet may also generate random numbers with a cell-formula.

Wycliffe's original device apparently had a single big wheel numbered from 0 to 180 and was spun three times to produce a random number.

PUBLISHER'S FORWARD

This book was found in research of plot generators and all things about how to write short stories.

Flash fiction has now replaced the Wycliff's original term "short-short story" in our age.

But the essential points of this form are the same:

- **Brief** - less than a thousand words, usually.

- **To the Point** – the sheer lack of space means usually staring in the middle of the action.

- **Effective** – a sparse word count means that every single word-choice counts to forward the plot, the character, or emotional response.

Other novels can ramble on for eighty-thousand words or more. But flash fiction has to leap full-armed from the brow of its creator, engaging and transforming.

In this book, we revive a quick method for inspiration, one which has consistently received rave reviews from its many fans, both in the 30's when first published and today.

Also included is a selection from Henry Albert Phillips', *The Plot of the Short Story*. Written two decades earlier than Hill's work, it covers the essential point of determining the "germ" of a story and then fleshing it out. The Plot Wizard will only give you the skeleton – it is up to you to know your audience and reward them for reading.

You have about 3-4 pages to do it.

Have fun with this.

THE FORMULA

Use a Random Number Generator ("Wizard" or "Genie")

Look up the Number Suggestions for:

1. Locale
2. Principal Character
3. Motivation
4. Obstacle
5. Method of Attack
6. Predicament or Crisis
7. The Climax

Write these out in full before you read the whole text.

Then let your inspiration take hold to tell you the whole story. (See full Instructions below.)

INTRODUCTION

The series of Plot Wizard Indices would not be complete without the addition of one which supplies the plot outline for the short-short (or "flash fiction") story—so popular has this type of fiction become in the past few years.

Not only is the "flash fiction" story popular with the reading public but on account of the fact that a number of enterprising publishers have offered unusually large financial compensation for such stories, thousands of authors have come to look upon it as a handy "pot boiler."

The Formula and Index differs from all of the others which accompany the Wizard. It may be said to be similar to all of them but unlike any. In reading and analyzing most of the "flash fiction"s that have been published in Liberty and Collier's for a period of two years, I found that they embrace all the plot types, and because of this it was necessary to devise a special formula which would give the author all the leeway necessary in dialing out the kind of plots he wanted.

Romantic melodrama, plain action-adventure, detective-mystery, comedy, or romance and pathos—all of them are at your disposal with the use of the following formula for the "flash fiction" Story. It all depends on whether you dial even or odd numbers—and in the treatment you give the resulting outline.

Wycliffe A. Hill

WHAT IS A "FLASH FICTION" STORY?

Although many authors will not acknowledge it as a fact, and others recognize it subconsciously or intuitively, while some openly admit it to be the method employed by them, all fiction story plots are mechanically constructed, after a pattern or a formula, by a system of rules or according to a specific design. The perfect plot must be just as carefully engineered as are the plans and blueprints of any great structure.

Ingredients of which all story plots are made are characters, situations, backgrounds and action. Persons involved in situations result in action, while background lends color. Of course, like snowflakes which form themselves into many varied and beautiful designs by accident of pattern, human incidents or events frequently shape themselves into story material.

I said that there is a formula for every type of story. So there is for everything else in the Universe. In order to discover it one must first analyze a considerable quantity of the material at hand, separate it into its constituent parts, ascertain the proportions used, the process or order of introduction and guess at the catalytic element or chemical action- which followed.

When I was confronted with the task of discovering the stuff of which "flash fiction" stories are made I naturally proceeded to do the thing first named in the previous paragraph. Fortunately I was able to obtain hack numbers of LIBERTY and COLLIER'S for about two years past.

Next, I read every "flash fiction" story in these magazines and reduced each to a synopsis of from a dozen to fifty words. These were pasted on strips of cardboard so they could be conveniently classified.

Then, I proceeded to make a list of the elements found in them, in the following order:

(I) The place, locale, or background.

(2) The principal character or characters.

(3) The primary motivation. of these characters.

(4) The obstacle.

(5) Manner of effort employed to overcome the main obstacle.

(6) The predicament or crisis which followed.

(7) The climax or climactic situation.

Each of these elements was identified and noted in the abstract, or by a general description such as would make possible its use in any story. The wealth of unusual climactic situations which were revealed was nothing short of amazing. Needless to say, I also discovered the "tricks" that various "flash fiction" story writers employ to introduce the "punch," "twist" or surprise ending.

My analysis shows that these gems of literature which have passed the critical eye of the editors of LIBERTY cover a wide range, not only as to type, but in the amount of plot and action which they contain, and the probable source of the material in them.

Not only are the majority of them "meaty" with dramatic situations and plot but many have been so beautifully written that they might properly be called masterpieces of dialogue and description. They differ from the ordinary short-story in that almost without exception the interest of the' reader is seized and the story under way at top speed in the first one hundred words or less. Each has a punch, twist, or surprise of some kind made possible by the clever handling of dialogue or situation, or delineation of character.

"TRICK" ENDINGS

One of the outstanding features of the short, short story and that which differentiates it from the ordinary short story is what is commonly called the "trick" ending embracing a surprise twist, a dramatic punch, a paradox, or a chuckle. This is accomplished by cleverly handling the description and dialogue in such a way that either or both may be possible of more than one interpretation or where there is a double meaning. Another method is to purposely withhold certain facts until. the last paragraph—thereby providing a surprise twist at the end.

The length of the "flash fiction" story varies from 500 to 2000 words although the popularly accepted idea is around 1000 words. It does not necessarily follow, however, that because a manuscript contains the specified number of words, it qualifies as a "flash fiction" Story. While being written in the accepted fiction style, and not a mere synopsis as the untrained writer might suppose, it must possess the other qualifications previously described if it is to meet with the editor's favor.

PRANKS OF FATE

We have still another type of "flash fiction" story which seems to be very popular and in which the main outstanding feature is occasioned by a prank of fate or wherein some unexpected thing, over which the characters in the story have no control, occurs thereby providing either a muse for action or a climax.

DIRECTIONS

Inasmuch as the "flash fiction" story embraces the various types of plots including romance, melodrama, pathos, and comedy, it has been necessary to arrange this Formula and Index in such a manner that the author may choose the type of plot outline he is going to dial out. If the outline for a romance, straight comedy, tragedy or heart interest character story is desired, one should dial for ODD numbers such as 1, 3, 5, 7, except in the matter of locales as it is immaterial whether an Even or an Odd number is dialed for them. If, on the other hand, one desires a plot outline for a melodrama, melodramatic romance, action-adventure. detective-mystery, or "hokum" comedy, one should dial for the EVEN numbers such as 2, 4, 6, 8 and so on, beginning with the list of characters using either even or odd for Locale.

The following special instructions will be found helpful:

1. If it is desired to dial a plot outline for romantic tragedy one may select from the lists and write in his own motivation. crisis and climax and dial for the other four, bearing in mind that he should dial for ODD numbers only. By selecting the three above-named elements one may determine the nature of the plot to be dialed out.

2. Should one desire to obtain a plot outline for melodrama of the action adventure type one may select the character. motivation and method of attack from the lists, write these in and dial for the other four elements.

By so doing the nature of the plot outline supplied can be determined in advance. Only EVEN numbers should be dialed for this.

3. Should one wish to write a "hokum" comedy he may select the principal character, the motivation and the climax from the lists, write them in and dial for the remaining four elements bearing in mind that only EVEN numbers should be dialed. After all, what is known as "hokum" comedy is nothing more nor less than exaggerated melodrama in which comic characters who have funny ideas are placed in ludicrous situations and either rescued or not.

4. Should it be desired to obtain a plot of the detective-mystery type one may choose from the lists the motivation, method of attack and the climax. Write these in and dial for the other four elements, bearing in mind that only EVEN numbers should be dialed. All detective-mystery stories are, of course, of the melodramatic type.

5. If it is desired to obtain a plot for a romance or simple love story without melodrama and in which heart interest is an important feature, one may select from the lists. motivation. the method of attack and the crisis. and dial for the other four elements. it being understood that ODD numbers only may be used. The simple love story deals with the proposition of the manner in which one or more obstacles which stand in the way of a love affair between two people are removed, or in case the story ends in a tragedy, deals with the efforts made to overcome the obstacle and the fatal result.

6. If one wishes to obtain a plot for the straight comedy or the comedy drama he may choose from the lists. motivation, crisis and climax and dial for the other elements. using ODD numbers only. A story of this kind must of course end happily. The predicament must also be more or less of a humorous nature to prevent the situation from becoming so serious that it develops into a heavy drama. In the former there are no serious dramatic situations although they may verge upon the dramatic. The latter may be the heaviest kind of drama in places but highlighted with comedy relief.

These special directions are given for the benefit of the author who desires to determine in advance what type of story plot outline is to be evolved. Of course. they may be disregarded entirely provided the author remembers the main ides that if certain types of plots are wanted EVEN numbers should be dialed, and if other types are wanted ODD numbers should be dialed.

GET YOUR NUMBERS FIRST

Dial out your seven numbers first and write them in on your Recording Sheet. Now write in the seven corresponding answers from the lists of story elements. This Will provide you with a story plot outline and assignment which will tell you where the story takes place—who the principal character is—what problem, or emotion motivates him—what outstanding obstacle stands in the way—what effort he puts forth or the method of attack employed to remove the obstacle—what predicament or crisis is precipitated—and the climactic situation which ends the story. In figuring out how to reconcile these various elements one with the other, it will be observed that if additional characters are necessary to the story they will automatically introduce themselves or be suggested. By the time one has done this he will also have a story plot.

Study the outline as a WHOLE, follow the same method of asking yourself questions as is shown in the development of the sample plot which follows. then write a brief synopsis of two or three hundred words. Go over this several times in search for illogical situations or action—or for loose ends or contradictory action or development; and if necessary, change the story to eliminate these imperfections. You will find the to be excellent practice in plot building.

You are now ready to give names to your characters insert some dialogue and descriptive background. This may or may not require the use of several thousand words. The next step in converting the short -story which you will now have into a "flash fiction" story will be to boil the whole thing down around the biggest situation in the story.

You will find that this will usually be around the climax; although during the mental process used in the development of the plot, there may be suggested an entirely new angle or idea which will supply the desired punch for your "flash fiction" story. Bear in mind the fact that your story must comply with these important requirements:

(1) You must seize the interest of the reader and get the story under way at top speed, with all principal characters introduced, in the first two hundred words.

(2) A strong thread of suspense must be established and maintained from the beginning to the and.

(3) There must be a surprise twist, dramatic or comic punch or a paradoxical climax in the last one hundred words.

(4) You must make every word tell something—situation, action, characterization or color.

DEVELOPING THE PLOT

We are now going to choose an outline for further development as example. We will begin a sample plot generated from the even numbers.

LOCALE	38	At a cabaret.
CHARACTER	133	A husband.
MOTIVATION	77	Desire to save the soul of a loved one.
OBSTACLE	105	False pride.
METHOD	131	Pathetic effort is made to eclipse another.
CRISIS	167	A great mistake is about to be made because of a dream.
CLIMAX	17	Wherein a little child is the means of bringing about a reconciliation.

This gives you a premise:

> *We open on a cabaret as a background or locale. One of the principal characters is a husband, and some one is motivated with a desire to save the soul of a loved one. False pride on the part of some character introduces a serious obstacle and there is a pathetic effort made to eclipse another. The crisis develops when a great mistake is about to be made because of a dream. This is followed by a climax wherein a little child is the means of bringing about a reconciliation.*

As previously explained in connection with this system of plot building, Wizard tells you WHAT happens and when you figure out HOW it could happen that way, you have a plot. The directions further advise one to study the outline as a WHOLE and to make a serious effort to reconcile the various story elements suggested, one with the other. This leads us to ask ourselves a number of questions—and when we find a satisfactory answer to than, die plot will have developed itself materially. let us see what we have to consider in the outline, which we are going to develop now.

My reader will of course understand that this is only one of scores of "flash fiction" story plots that could be evolved from this outline. And it was developed in less than fifteen minutes.

You should ask yourself the journalist's questions of "who, what, when, where, why, and how?"

These might be as follows:

1. Where is the cabaret located?

2. What is the husband doing in the cabaret? ' 3. Whose husband is he?

4. What is his profession?

5. Who is the loved one whose soul is to be saved?

6. In what way is the soul about to be lost?

7. How is it proposed to save the soul?

8. Is the lost soul a man or a woman?

9. Is the lost soul any relation to the husband?

10. What relation?

11. Who is possessed of false pride?

12. Who makes the pathetic effort to eclipse another?

13. In what way is the effort made?

14. Who is the other one?

15. Why is the effort pathetic?

16. What kind of a mistake is about to made on account of a dream?

17. Who is about to make the mistake?

18. Who is the dreamer?

19. What was the dream?

20. How could a dream cause the mistake?

21. How does a little child bring about a reconciliation?

22. Between whom is a reconciliation effected?

23. What has been the cause of the rift between the parties who become reconciled?

24. What relation is the child to the parties who become reconciled?

25 . Is the husband one of the parties who become reconciled?

26. If so, with whom does he become reconciled?

27. Is the child any relation to the husband?

28. If so, what?

As we flesh out our synopsis, our imagination fills in the answers:

A young woman who has been a dancer becomes the wife of a more or less prosaic or commonplace husband whose position some time later places him in contact with a radio station. It is discovered that he has natural ability as a singer. He is given a few tryouts, takes training and soon becomes a star baritone.

The couple have a little girl three or four years old and being the wife of a star, whose time and attention are largely monopolized by other people, soon becomes burdensome to die wife. Having been a dancer she has some professional ambition which never forsakes her and she takes seriously the remarks made by some of her friends about the attention paid to her husband by other women.

Professional engagements take the husband away for a time and the wife places the little girl in the care of a friend and resolves to make a name for herself in the professional world. The first opportunity that presents itself is in a night club. The husband returns and is shocked. He goes to the nightclub and pleads with her to give up the idea and she proudly refuses. He sees that she is in an atmosphere that may prove to be ruinous. She can think of nothing but her consuming ambition to become his equal professionally or to perhaps eclipse him. He tells her that she is going to the devil. This results in an estrangement.

For a time he makes veiled appeals to her over the radio as he sings to his audience. She gets the messages but does not heed them.

Then comes a time when he in the broadcasting studio hears the announcer describe an accident to an unidentified child who has been run down by an automobile and he recognizes it as his own. In the midst of a gay number at the cabaret she hears the same announcement and with a cry dashes from the stage. The two meet at the bedside of the injured tot at the hospital and silently pray for her life. The child hovers between life and death for days during which time all misunderstandings between the mother and the father are melted away and when the child recovers consciousness she sees them in each other's arms. When the father asks the little one how she came to run away and be injured she replies: "I dreamed the devil was after my mama and I was going down to get her."

The End.

While this is still short of what could be done with a full thousand words, it's example shows how the Plot Wizard can help you quickly fire your imagination and inspiration.

It is more difficult to write a heart interest drama than it is a melodrama and even though this little story appears to have less plot in it than the other one, more mental effort has been required to write it so as to include the necessary heart interest and pathos as well as the dramatic punch at the end.

Attention is directed here to the difference between the trick ending or surprise twist which is found in the other story, and the dramatic punch or heart throb which we have at the end of this one. Here we have not purposely reserved any pertinent facts, introduced misleading dialogue, or had any character do some unexpected thing at the last minute in order to provide the trick ending or surprise twist. Instead we have simply used the child's statement of her dream about her mother as the climax. There is heart interest in this for the reason that it emphasizes the love of the child for her mother and establishes the fact that she has perhaps overheard the father's statement that the mother is "going to the devil" and has taken it seriously. To have introduced the statement of the child earlier in this way would have been to have lost the dramatic punch and heart interest climax at the end. All of which goes to show that the way in which one tells the story is as important as the story itself.

Right here it might be well to emphasize the fact that the Plot Wizard is not designed to supply the continuity for a story. but merely a plot outline.

In other words, it's not necessary that the introduction of story elements appear in the same order or even a similar order in the finished story as they do in the plot outline. The Wizard is intended to supply the plot and then the author can tell the story in any manner desired. One must first have a story before he can tell it however and to supply this story is the purpose of the Plot Wizard.

THE LISTS

CHARACTERS

1. An old peddle.

2. A police officer

3. A fisherman's daughter

4. A Shylock

5. A waitress

6. A roue

7. An eat/wife

8. A sheriff

9. A cabaret girl

10. A bully

11. A negro mammy

12. A smuggler

1 3. A blind beggar

14. A thief

15. A small boy (or child)

16. A detective

17. An old maid

18. A gangster

19. A watchman

20. A counterfeiter

21. A mine operator

22. An Arab

23. A newspaperman

24. An army officer

25. A captain

26. A spy

27. A lineman

28. A paramour

29. A rich old man

30. A member of the Black Hand

31. A young doctor

32. A playboy

33. A stenographer

34. An old hag

35. A divorcée

36. A caballero

37. An ex-husband

38. A gambler

39. A society leader

40. A bandit

41. A saleslady

42. A vice lord

43. An old employee

44. A duelist

45'. A fisherman

46. A moonshine:

47. An announcer

48. An ex-servant

49. A hunter

50. A cowboy

51. A nurse

52. A dancer

53. An athlete

54. A wife

55. An old farmer

56. A country woman

57. A young farmer lad

58. A magician

59. A seaman

60. A pugilist

61. An executive

62. A fugitive

63. A trainer

64. A promoter

65. A rancher

66. A soldier

67. A society girl

68. A twin

69. An office clerk

70. A working girl

71. A poor girl

72. A chauffeur

73. A small merchant

74. A rich farmer

75. A farm hand

76. A merchant prince

77. An actor

78. A guide

79. A henpecked husband

80. A young negro

81. A neglected wife

82. A girl reporter

83. A performer

84. A waiter

85. A technician

86. A scientist

87. An inventor

88. A politician

89. A confidence man

90. A bank clerk

91. A fireman

92. A warden

93. A widow

94. A consul

95. A scrub-woman

96. A trader

97. A telegrapher

98. An interpreter

99. A pretender

100. An heir

101. A derelict

102. An heiress

103. A playwright

104. A failure

105. An actress

106. A producer

107. A recruit

108. A jokester

109. An operator

110. A weakling

111. A teacher

112. A business rival

113. A photographer

114. A vagabond

115. A pilot

116. A gigolo

117. An artist

118. A soldier of fortune

119. A ranger

120. A ne'er-do-well

121. An editor

122. A chemist

123. A laborer

124. A doctor

125. An invalid

126. An aviator

127. A governess

128. A rival in love

129. A press agent

130. An acrobat

131. A young modem

132. A smuggler

133. A husband

134. A dance hall girl

135. An old woman

136. A crook

137. An old family servant

138. A forget

139. A and sharp

140. A society dame

141. A servant

142. A night club hostess

143. A farmer's daughter

144. A dope peddler

145. A boatman

146. A taxi driver

147. A gypsy

148. A mystic

149. A ranch owner

150. A hermit

151. A shepherd

152. A jockey

153. A writer

154. A taxidermist

155. A plastic surgeon

156. A hypnotist

157. A manufacturer

158. A diver

159. A journalist

160. A prosecutor

161. An adventuress

162. An interne

163. A girl clerk

164. An animal trainer

165. A prince

166. A judge

167. A sport star

168. A Hindu

169. A driller

170. A bouncer

171. An immigrant man

172. A model

173. A miner

174. A bacteriologist

175. A collegian

176. A railroader

177. An immigrant girl

178. A bus driver

179. A gypsy girl

180. A Secret Service operative

LOCALE

1. Aboard ship.

2. By a lake

3. At the Casino

4. In an Abbey

5. In the oil fields

6. In a palatial home

7. At the harbor

8. In school

9. In the Far North

10. In India

11. In a love nest

12. At an Army post

13. In Latin America

14. In a shack

15 . In a colony

16. In a light house

17. At a saw mill

18. In the marshes

19. At the morgue

20. In a factory district

21. On a dude ranch

22. At a damp meeting

23. Behind the footlights

24. On the Bowery

25. In an office

26. At a depot

27. On a sugar plantation

28. In a refugee amp

29. At a resort

30. At a hospital

31. On a Bayou

32. In a tenement

33. On the farm

34. On a country estate

35. At the sea coast

36. On a race track

37. In a print shop

38. At a cabaret

39. On a sheep ranch

40. On a small farm

41. In a ball room

42. In the underworld

43. In Dixie

44. In a fishing village

45 . In a pirate hangout

46. At an arsenal

47. On a ranch

48. In the rice fields

49. At the Mardi Gras

50. At a roadhouse

51. In an explorer's camp

52. At a convention

53. In a department store

54. In a coliseum

55. On a tobacco plantation

56. In a small town

57. On a battlefield

58. In the retail district

59. In the countryside

60. In court

61. In a shop

62. In the North Woods

63. At a gambling resort

64. In a corporation office

65. In a bachelor's apartment

66. On the desert

67. At a party (or celebration)

68. By a river

69. In Egypt

70. On a beach

71. In a newspaper office

72. In a bank

73. In the slums

74. At a masque ball

75. In a small town hotel

76. In college

77. In the tropics

78. On an island

79. At a mission

80. At steel mills

81. In the jungle

82. On a yacht

83. In a mining town

84. In an asylum

85. On the golf-links

86. On the plains

87. In a curio shop

88. In a castle

89. On the prairie

90. In Mexico

91. One. freighter

92. In a vineyard

93. In a caravan

94. In a foundry

95. At the altar

96. At a. dam site

97. In Arabia

98. In a haunted house

99. At a mine

100. In a questionable house

101. On a distant frontier

102. At a police station

103. On the sea

104. On the Amazon

105. In prison

106. In a park

107. In the cane brake

108. On a cotton plantation

109. In a movie studio

110. On the highway

111. In a wireless station

112. In the mountains

113. At a fort

114. In a middle class home

115. At an airport

116. In Africa

117. At a hacienda

118. At a field hospital

119. In the Navy

120. In a penthouse

121. At a theater

122. In the legislature

123. Backstage.

124. At a circus

125. At Police headquarters

126. In pine woods

127. At a logging camp

128. In a dope den

129. In a back settlement

130. In an airplane

131. In a swamp

132. In a cheap boarding house.

133. At a hotel

134. In an orchard

135. In the Orient

136. In a canyon

137. In an encampment

138. Out West

139. At railroad yards

140. Aboard a train

141. In the forest

142. In a deserted house

143. At a banquet

144. In a paper mill

145. In the financial district

146. On a wagon train

147. In the South Sm

148. In a bandit amp .

149. At a camp

150. In a factory

151. On city streets

152. Down East

153. In a construction camp

154. In the trenches

156. In an artist's studio

157. In China

158. In a museum

159. In Asia

160. At a festival

161. In a dance hall

162. On a gambling ship

163. In a taxi.

164. In a gypsy camp

165. In the Far East

166. At a country inn

167. In grain fields

168. In a laboratory

169. In a savage country

170. On a plantation

171. In an academy

172. In the poor house

173. On a game preserve

174. At a radio station

175. On a river

176. In Hawaii

177. In an arena

178. In the war zone

179. At a lonely outpost

180. In a flotilla

MOTIVATION

1. Desire to save an unfortunate from an indiscretion.

2. Desire for an illicit love.

3. Desire to conceal one's dishonor from a loved one.

4. Revenge against one who has exposed perfidy.

5. Desire to protect one's self against a bully.

6. To place one's crime at the door of another.

7. Desire to achieve position or fame.

8. Desire to visit a secret revenge on an enemy.

9. Desire to penetrate the secrets of another.

10. Desire to escape the result of one's own perfidy.

11. Desire to reform a loved one.

12. Revenge desired against intruders.

13. Desire to prove one's loyalty.

14. Desire to remove a dangerous witness.

15. Desire to show off.

16. An unholy impulse to do something wrong for experimental purposes.

17. Desire to leave one's record clear.

18. Impulse to save a kinsman from enemies.

19. Desire to see a loved one make good.

20. Desire to protect a professional reputation.

21. Desire to be forgiven by a loved one who has been wronged.

22. Revenge against one who has wronged a loved one.

23. Desire to win sympathy.

24. Desire to save one's own life.

25. Desire to make atonement for the wrongs done by a kinsman or loved one.

26. Desire for money.

27. Desire to secretly assist another.

28. Desire to bribe an officer.

29. Desire to drown a sorrow.

30. Desire to preserve a professional record.

31. Desire to satisfy a. whim.

32. Desire to punish a scoundrel.

33. Desire to establish a precedent or record.

34. Desire to avenge a loved one's death.

35. Desire to provide a valuable possession for a loved one.

36. Desire to outwit or trap a bully.

37. Desire to make a success of one's business or profession.

38. Desire to escape the toils of the enemy.

39. Desire to prove one's self worthy.

40. Desire to conceal the evidence of one's crime.

41. Desire to sacrifice one's self for one who has a better right.

42. Desire to seek revenge against a rival.

43. Desire to escape grief or remorse.

44. Revenge sought against a deceiver.

45. Desire to reward faithful performance.

46. Overzealous desire to enforce a law.

47. Desire to ingratiate one's self with authority.

48. Desire to outwit a tyrant.

49. Desire to be near a worshiped one.

50. Desire to outwit a rival.

51. Desire to escape a tiresome experience or person.

52. Desire to avenge one's self against an old enemy.

53. Desire to display one's generosity or other virtue.

54. Desire to find a place of concealment for stolen valuables.

55. Desire to save one's self from a rash act.

56. Desire to escape the advances of another.

57. Desire to escape the reproaches of a loved one.

58. Desire to protect the name of a deceased loved one.

59. Desire to prove one's art or science.

60. Desire to give a rascal a dose of his own medicine.

61. Desire to nullify the machinery of the law.

62. Desire to prevent wholesale disgrace.

63. Desire to impress a member of the opposite sex.

64. Desire to outwit would be murderers.

65'. Desire to escape a hated responsibility.

66. Desire to nullify the machinery of the law.

67. Desire to be near a loved one.

68. Desire to outwit a lawless gang.

69. Desire to vindicate the word of another.

70. Desire to escape an unknown danger.

71. Desire to secretly observe another person.

72. Desire to escape a vicious animal or reptile.

73. Desire to secretly observe an operation of any kind.

74. Desire to bribe a trusted employee.

75 . Desire to save one's self.

76. Desire to trap a love thief.

77. Desire to save the soul of a loved one.

78. Desire to prove one's bravery.

79. Desire to escape temptation.

80. Desire to trick one into a confession.

81. Desire to remove temptation from the way of a dear one.

82. Desire to save one's property or valuables.

83. Desire to solve a mystery.

84. Desire to signal for help.

85. Desire to avoid a tragic accident or catastrophe.

86. Desire to obtain revenge against one who has violated an oath.

87. Desire to avoid the consequences of a natural phenomenon.

88. Punishment sought against a deceiver.

89. Desire to win a following.

90. Desire to punish a blackmailer.

91. Desire to escape a dangerous mission.

92. A plan to pursue revenge against a public enemy.

93. Desire to escape a bad habit.

94. Apprehension and punishment of a kidnapper is sought.

95. Desire to avoid the appearance of evil.

96. Desire to quell a revolt or uprising.

97. Desire to conceal one's indiscretions from a loved one.

98. Prevention of a boycott is sought.

99. Desire to rescue a loved one from a bad habit.

100. Desire to suppress a fraud.

101. Desire to save dear ones from the consequences of a natural phenomenon.

102. To combat an ignorant belief.

103. Desire to destroy a superstition.

104. Desire to enforce the orders of a superior.

105. Desire to convert a loved one.

106. To combat a vicious animal.

107. Desire to remedy a misunderstanding.

108. To monopolize attention.

109. Desire to prevent a misunderstanding.

110. To deprive an enemy of authority.

111. Desire to prevent an injustice.

112. To get a signal through.

113. Desire to obtain a valuable secret.

114. To expose the bluff of an enemy.

115. Desire to rescue an unfortunate.

116. To discredit the credentials of a person.

117. Desire to save one's home.

118. To disprove the charges of a blackmailer.

119. Desire to escape inclement weather.

120. To prove one mentally incompetent.

121. Desire to escape a baneful influence.

122. To prevent an abduction.

123. Desire to recover lost valuables.

124. To save one from a disastrous marriage.

125. Desire to avoid suspicion.

126. To bring about a desired match for money.

127. Desire to identify a strange person.

128. To punish a guilty kinsman.

129. Desire to identify a mysterious thing.

130. To win a valuable monetary reward.

131. Desire to win the love of the opposite sex.

132. Desire to escape vengeance.

133. Desire to win approbation of the public.

134. To outwit a conspirator.

135. To win the approbation of a superior.

136. Plan to expose a vicious ring.

137. To achieve a business success.

138. To protect a throne from overthrow.

139. To win professional achievement.

140. To reveal a plot against authority.

141. To protect one's good name.

142. To escape from bad company.

143. To protect the good name of a loved one.

144. To smuggle a valuable object.

145. To win the love of a kinsman.

146. Desire to crush a rival.

147. Desire to test the faith of a loved one.

148. Desire to uncover hidden wealth.

149. Desire to win the love of a friend.

150. To spy on an enemy.

151. Desire to establish a reconciliation with a loved one.

152. To east suspicion on another.

153. Desire to escape false accusation.

154. To frighten an enemy.

155. Desire to prove one's loyalty to country.

156. To turn enemies against one another.

157. Desire reconciliation with an associate.

158. To interfere with the plans of a rival.

159. Desired recovery of health.

160. To deceive a rival or enemy.

161. Desire to settle a feud.

162. To bribe one who is an obstacle.

163. Great fame desired.

164. To gain political power.

165. Relief from an ill desired.

166. To overthrow an Oppressor.

167. Recovery of the health of a loved one desired,

168. To conceal an embarrassing object.

169. To test the faith of an employee.

170. To obtain revenge against a race or clan.

171. Desire to make a loved one happy.

172. Desire to obtain revenge against an insulter.

173. The approbation of the opposite sex.

174. Vengeance sought against a robber.

175. Escape from ennui desired.

176. Vengeance sought against one who has defrauded.

177. Relief from pursuit desired.

178. Desire to punish one who has damaged good name.

179. To obtain a desired possession.

180. Pursuit sought against a law breaker.

THE OBSTACLE

1. The pride of a loved one.

2. An overpowering influence.

3. A troublesome habit.

4. The fact that one is guilty.

5. A guilty conscience.

6. Lack of a means of escape.

7. A mistake in the identity of an object.

8. One is confined in a dangerous place.

9. One's intentions are misunderstood.

10. The honor of another is involved.

11. An innocent party stands in the way.

12. An obsession.

13. A miscarriage of plans.

14. An overzealous disposition.

15. The indifference of Others.

16. An unfounded suspicion.

17. The persistence of another.

18. The vengeance of old enemies.

19. Failure of perception of another.

20. The interference of the law.

21. Failure to convince or impress others.

22. The handicap of evil associates.

23. An old Will or decree.

24. The presence of a sinister influence.

25. Failure of someone to appear.

26. The fatal ambition of another.

27. A bashful nature.

28. A secret relationship.

29. A suspicious disposition.

30. A mental malady.

31. A rival favored by opportunity.

32. The necessity of concealing an identity.

33. A physical disability.

34. A physical cowardice.

35 . A mistake in the identity of a situation.

36. A moral cowardice.

37. A secret responsibility.

38. A secret and vicious association.

39. A former relationship.

40. The unexpected presence of a detecting apparatus.

41. A duty to a loved one.

42. One's liberty is curtailed.

.43. An innocent misunderstanding.

44. The infatuation of a character.

45. An ignorance based on innocence.

46. A good for nothing relative.

47. Mistaken jealousy.

48. A matter of honor or principle.

49. One's ability or worth is discounted.

50. An unwelcome cynosure.

51. One's ability is unrecognized.

52. Lack of an implement, tool, or facilities.

53. A difference in status.

54. A dangerous adventure is involved.

55. Duty to country.

56. The presence of a threatener.

57. A consuming grief.

58. A secret desire for revenge.

59. A mistake in the identity of a person or people.

60. Threatened pursuit by officers of the law.

61. The attitude of a pessimist.

62. The lack of desirable opportunity.

63. The attitude of a hard-boiled cynic.

64. The near proximity of the enemy.

65. The presence of a deceiver.

66. The danger of causing a serious alarm.

67. The operation of a subconscious mind.

68. The lack of a method of signaling.

69. The welfare of a loved one.

70. The necessity of restoring one's liberty.

71. The fear of one's own weakness.

72. The obligation to risk one's honor.

73. The strict ideas of a loved one.

74. The necessity of risking the loss of friendship.

75. The annoyance of an insignificant thing.

76. Because one is under suspicion.

77. The ignorance of another.

78. Because one is already involved with the law.

79. The opposition of friends.

80. Because one is a fugitive.

81. The lack of privacy.

82. The danger of arousing the vengeance of an organization.

83. The lack of understanding.

84. The possible loss of one's liberty.

85. The innocent interference of a loved one.

86. The danger of losing a loved one.

87. One's own pride.

88. Threatened disaster to a loved one.

89. A distracting incident.

90. The unwillingness to face a serious issue.

91. A difference in skill.

92. The loyalty of a friend must be tested.

93. Inclement weather.

94. The watchfulness of a rival.

95. The matter of distance.

96. The possession of incorrect information or direction.

97. Parental objection.

98. The danger of occult interference.

99. A spiritual influence.

100. The suspicion that one is being tricked.

101. A previous agreement or contract.

102. The danger of precipitating a boycott.

103. One's credulity or unsophistication.

104. Lack of money.

105. False pride.

106. Lack of facilities.

107. Fear of exposure.

108. Lack of means of transportation.

109. The conversation of another.

110. The leaving of a task unperformed.

111. The failure to be convinced.

112. The necessity of becoming associated with a fugitive.

113. Handicapped by position.

114. The desire for vengeance.

115. An unscrupulous rival.

116. The rivalry of a kinsman.

117. The necessity of remaining silent.

118. The possible pursuit of the law.

119. A misplaced confidence.

120. The necessity of taking orders from a crook.

121. A disillusionment.

122. To be blocked by stormy weather.

123. The fear of a jealous rival.

124. The appearance of a mysterious woman.

125. An accusation of being untrue.

126.- The safety of a child.

127. Because one is not recognized.

128. Possible pursuit by a rival.

129. There is a difference of race.

130. The threat of a blackmailer.

131. There is an imaginary past.

132. The presence of a deceiver.

133. An innocent believed himself to be guilty.

134. Threatened loss of possession.

135. One is not taken seriously.

136. An unwritten law.

137. One is accused of being mentally deranged.

138. An intense jealousy on the part of another.

139. There is an imaginary difference of race.

140. The envy of a person.

141. A difference in religion or belief.

142. The disloyalty of a friend.

143. One has been forgotten.

144. A false accusation.

145 . The endurance of one is questioned.

146. The danger of incurring the enmity of kinsmen.

147. The loyalty of one is in doubt.

148. The possibility of losing one's good name.

149. The matter of pride stands in the way.

150. The jealousy of a wife or sweetheart.

151. Persons are on opposite legal sides.

15 2. The leaving of a treasure unprotected.

153. Opposition is offered by children.

154. The threatened disloyalty of an employee.

155. One's intentions are impugned.

156. The necessity to discover the identity of a mysterious character.

157. Persons are professional rivals.

158. The necessity of keeping a plan a secret.

159. The violation of a principle is threatened.

160. A strange code or clue must be discovered.

161. Financial loss impends.

162. The reluctance to become associated with a crook.

163. A solemn vow stands in the way.

164. A foolish superstition.

165. Duty to a loved one stands in the way.

166. An ambition for power.

167. There is a difference in rank.

168. One is enslaved by a habit.

169. An unhappy marriage is an obstacle.

170. Persons are political rivals or enemies.

171. Persons are members of enemy clans.

172. A person has a fatal ambition for wealth.

173. One is threatened with the necessity of solving a mystery.

174. The opposition of enemies.

175. Persons are shamed to be associated together.

176. The danger of precipitating a revolt.

177. A traditional custom stands in the way.

178. A hateful indebtedness to another.

179. An ancestral decree is an obstacle.

180. One is being watched by a spy.

METHOD OF ATTACK

1. Imperiling a social position.

2. Personal encounter.

3. Creation of an imaginary person to deceive.

4. Some one is bribed.

5. The use of sex appeal.

6. Spurred to a daring effort.

7. Giving of secret aid.

8. Making a promise which has a double meaning.

9. The use of suggestion.

10. The making of a surprise sacrifice or revenge.

11. Indulge in a counter attraction.

12. The voluntary assumption of a dangerous or ridiculous position.

13. A relationship breached.

14. The decision to take one's own life.

15. The use of persuasion.

16. Escaping by flight.

17. Taking advantage of another's handicap.

18. The daring of fate to restore self-confidence.

19. The use of action to frighten.

20. The laying of a trap.

21. A concession asked for the sake of an old friendship or love.

22. The use of a secret formula or scientific discovery.

23. The making of a last effort to prove one's self worthy.

24. Feigning suicide, death, or injury.

25 . The overriding of convention.

26. Quick disposal of an incriminating object or body.

27. The refusal to recognize an imposition.

28. Spying on the actions-of another.

29. The application of an art in which one is especially skilled.

30. A dangerous criminal experiment is planned or contemplated.

31. The necessity of deceiving a loved one is recognized.

32. A secret entrance is sought.

33. One resorts to flattery.

34. It is planned to establish a bold precedent.

35. Valuable or important information is withheld.

36. An unexpected reappearance is planned.

37. It is planned for one to take the place of another.

38. It is planned to place a secret mark of identification on a person.

39. An appeal is made to credulity or ignorance.

40. An appeal is made to superstition.

41. A figment of the imagination is told for effect.

42. A surprise clue or evidence is sought.

43. A gain sacrifice is made or contemplated.

44. A loved one is offered in sacrifice.

45. An effort is made to belittle or ridicule, or put to shame another.

46. A flogging is administered.

47. One offers servility to another.

48. A drug is administered.

49. A secret sacrifice is planned or offered.

50. Plan to commit arson.

51. A disguise is penetrated.

52. A kidnapping is planned.

53. A sudden disguise is effected.

54. A forgery is planned.

75. It is sought to trick 3. trickster.

56. A robbery or theft is planned.

57. It is planned to take advantage of a mistaken identity.

58. A dual role is enacted.

59. A spiritual assistant is sought.

60. It is planned to use a surprise weapon.

61. An appeal made for sympathy.

62. A mysterious advertisement is inserted.

63. A witness is secreted.

64. A misrepresentation is made as to one's age.

65. Advantage is taken of one who knows himself to be guilty.

66. A drug or chemical is used.

67. An appeal is made to filial or blood-relationship love.

68. An appeal is made to the underworld.

69. Valuable presents are offered.

70. A chemical analysis is made.

71. A compromise is offered.

72. An anesthetic is used.

73. An inspiration is sought.

74. Hypnotism is used.

75. It is planned to submit to bodily injury.

76. A secret hiding place is constructed.

77. It is planned to substitute one person for another.

78. One is lured to the haunts of criminals.

79. A clever substitution of objects is planned.

80. Mysterious baggage is concealed in trunks.

81. It is planned to cause a misunderstanding.

82. A strange emblem or symbol is placed as a signal.

83. A clever impersonation is planned.

84. A plan of action is abandoned for effect.

85. The use of twins or similar persons planned to confuse.

86. The use of fire is employed.

87. A clever play is made on sympathy.

88. Flight is attempted by way of ship, train, plane, or bus.

89. Detection by trick questioning.

90. A strict policy of silence is employed.

91. The assumption of a new identity.

92. A person is sent away on a mysterious trip.

93. A secret message sent for aid.

94. Marks are made to serve as a decoy.

95. The complete reversal of position.

96. A weapon is hidden.

97. An appeal made to vanity.

98. A murder is attempted.

99. The enactment of a clever role.

100. Arson is attempted.

101. The use of or attempt at a clever trick to still for time.

102. A kidnapping is attempted.

103. To hide or place one's self inconspicuously.

104. A forgery is attempted.

105. The exercise of supreme self-control under trying circumstances.

106. A peculiar accident is caused.

107. An imaginary rival is introduced for effect.

108. Evidence is concealed.

109. A journey is made.

110. A wrong address is given.

111. A promise is broken.

112. Attempt at blackmail.

113. The obstacle is ignored at great danger.

114. The concealment of evidence.

115. Daring effort is made for a thing of little consequence.

116. An appeal made to the law.

117. A secret identity is unexpectedly revealed.

118. The use of political influence.

119. A misunderstanding is cleverly arranged.

120. A sacrifice of money.

121. An appeal is made to honor or principle.

122. An appeal made to a religious creed, tradition or principle.

123. A daring offer is made to prove one's honor.

124. Confusing the enemy as to one's identity.

127. An appeal is made to filial or brotherly love.

126. A novel and unexpected signal for help.

127. Forgiveness is offered.

128. The use of open defiance against authority.

129. An offer is made to accept punishment to save another.

130. The use of violence.

1 31. Pathetic effort is made to eclipse another.

132. Heroic effort to stop panic.

133. Force is used to make an impression.

134. A villain is exposed.

135. Strategy is employed to prove an identity.

136. Capture is invited.

137. A real identity is purposely concealed.

138. Murder is planned in the guise of accident.

139. The use of bargaining to obtain a decision.

140. Armed opposition from a place of concealment.

141. The use of argument to obtain evidence.

142. A person is waylaid.

143. The use of ruse or strategy to attract attention.

144. The enemy is disarmed.

145. Using force to win sympathy.

146. There is a clever disguise of a signal. .

147. Using strategy to surprise.

148. Demoralization by an unexpected show of strength.

149. The use of force to mystify.

150. Weapons are captured.

151. The use of strategy to delay.

152. Reinforcements are cut out.

153. The use of argument to prove identity.

154. A clever trap is set.

155. The use of strategy to frighten.

156. A person is discredited.

157. The use of bargaining to hasten action.

158. Personal combat with weapons.

159. The use of strategy to uncover a due or evidence.

160. A machine is captured.

161. Bargaining to silence.

162. A clever scientific weapon is used.

163. Ruse to establish rights.

169. Supplies are withheld or waylaid.

165. Using force to prove strength.

166. An ignorant person is bribed.

167. Offering a sacrifice to prove loyalty.

168. There is a flight overland.

169. Using strategy to conceal.

170. There is a pursuit of a fugitive.

171. Resorting to ruse to allure.

172. A position is fortified.

173. The telling of an innocent lie to confuse.

174. The surrender of forces is agreed upon.

175. The use of entreaty to frustrate.

176. There is a raid from the air.

177. The use of bargaining to proselyte.

178. A messenger is intercepted.

179. The use of force to humble.

180. There is an appeal to the law.

PREDICAMENT OR CRISIS

1. About to lose one's eyesight.

2. A threatened loss of a loved one.

3. About to be superseded by a subordinate.

4. Threatened death at the hands of one who has been wronged.

5. About to lose a long-promised reward.

6. Death threatened by an indiscretion.

7. The death of a loved one is threatened.

8. Exposure threatened by one who has been wronged.

9. The loss of honor or virtue is threatened by a deceiver.

10. Arrest and detection imminent.

11. One is about to lose valuable property.

12. About to be slugged.

13. Stolen goods, concealed, are about to be uncovered.

14. One is tempted to take his own life.

15. Secreted evidence of value is about to be-uncovered.

16. One's life is secretly threatened by a rival.

17. An innocent person is about to unwittingly expose one.

18. An innocent, mistaken for a criminal, is about to be slain.

19. Caught in a compromising position, one's reputation is threatened.

20. Overzealous law enforcement threatens one's life.

21. One is about to be compelled to undertake the impossible.

22. One's life is threatened by an infatuated person.

23. One is about to overlook a marvelous opportunity.

24. An innocent is about to be framed by a guilty person.

25. Disgrace of a loved one is threatened.

26. One is about to give way to a criminal impulse.

27. One is about to fall into a trap.

28. One is about to wreak vengeance against an innocent person.

29. One is about to fall victim to superstition.

30. Misfortune is threatened by one's disclosing his plans to an enemy in disguise.

31. One is about to lose an important wager.

32. One is about to become a victim of a custom, tradition or oath.

33. One's motives are misunderstood by those whom he would befriend.

34. One is threatened with robbery and death.

35. One is prevented from rescuing a loved one who is threatened.

36. One is about to be attacked by a maniac.

37. A mistaken identity is about to frighten one into a rash act.

38. One is about to receive a flogging at the hands of a bully.

39. The habit of forgetfulness threatens to cause a misfortune.

40. One is about to fall prey to a mental malady.

41. Because of having lied, one is involved in serious consequences.

42. One has permitted himself to be used as a dupe or tool.

43. One is about to make a confession to a hypocrite who feigns sympathy.

44. One is threatened with blackmail.

45. One is about to be seriously involved by the wayward acts of a kinsman.

46. A supposed friend and follower is an enemy in disguise.

47. One is about to permit a hot temper to cause a rash act.

48. A loved one is about to fall into a trap for another.

49. Having breached relations with a loved one a person finds a substitution infinitely worse.

50. A trap is about to be sprung prematurely.

51. It is discovered that one has overdone a thing so that an opposite effect is created.

52. One's life or liberty is threatened by a gang.

53. One discovers he has been buncoed by a designing and clever- rascal.

54. One's guilt is about to be disclosed by an unexpected witness.

55. One falls prey to the sex attraction of an enemy.

56. Two characters secretly plot one another's death or ruin.

57. A mistaken identity has caused one to desert.

58. A love done is about to be injured or slain by one's own vile associates.

59. One is confronted with the apparent infidelity of a beloved one.

60. Fear of disaster compels one to keep secret his identity.

61. One is repulsed or spurned by another who is loved.

62. One is threatened with losing his spoils to another.

63. Two rivals or opponents are placed where only one can survive.

64. One is placed in jeopardy by the necessity of donning a disguise.

65'. One is about to break or lose a perfect record.

66. One is marked or branded in a. way that threatens misfortune.

67. Valuable testimony which will save one, is refused.

68. One is tempted to accept a bribe.

69. Through misunderstanding, one is about to desert a loved one.

70. Disaster is threatened by an epidemic.

71. A secret past is about to be disclosed to a loved one.

72. Mental derangement is threatened.

73. One is about to permit an insignificant obstacle to bring about downfall or failure.

74. Disaster is threatened by a revolt.

75. The indiscretion of a kinsman threatens to bring misfortune to one.

76. The loss of honor of a loved one is threatened.

77. One is accused of being a coward or weakling.

78. Banishment of a loved one is threatened.

79. Bashfulness or timidity threatens loss of victory.

80. One is about to slay an unrecognized kinsman.

81. One is about to have the "tables turned" on him.

82. One is about to permit a loved one who is unrecognized to perish.

83. One is threatened with great embarrassment.

84. Disaster is threatened by an explosion.

85. A loved one must be sacrificed to prevent exposure.

86. A good name is threatened by a blackmailer.

87. The good name of a departed friend or loved one is threatened.

88. One is about to lose his own life.

89. One is threatened with expulsion or banishment.

90. One is about to be obliged to sacrifice a loved one to the law.

91. One is about to witness a loved one suffer defeat.

92. One is about to take his own life.

93. A new friend or loved one threatens to desert to old associations.

94. It becomes necessary to surrender a loved one or kinsman to the law.

95. Loss of home is threatened.

96. A would be suicide is confronted with the problem of saving his own life.

97. Banishment is threatened.

98. Crooked politics deprive one of justice.

99. There is a threatened loss of position.

100. One is threatened with disgrace in his profession.

101. Loss of a reward of a loved one is threatened.

102. One is about to be kidnapped by a gang.

103. One is about to be disfigured.

104. One has committed a "faux pas" in official circles.

105. Misfortune is threatened by inclement weather.

106. One is surrounded by former evil associates whom he has deserted.

107. The loss of life of a loved one is threatened.

108. One is threatened with death if he does not perform the execution of a criminal commission.

109. A mistaken identity precipitates horror or terror.

110. One is forced to be an accomplice to a criminal.

111. One is about to be shanghaied.

112. One is about to be forced by a kinsman into becoming a criminal.

113. One has innocently amused an insane jealousy.

114. One is threatened by an avaricious person.

115. One is threatened by a vicious animal or reptile.

116. Sacrifice to passion, habit or mania threatens loss of relief.

117. One is threatened with disillusionment.

118. Parties desiring valuable information threaten abduction.

119. One has committed a "faux pas" in love or society.

120. An innocent person is avowed of having committed a crime.

121. One has been seriously mislead by the presence of twins or a mistaken identity of persons.

122. Parties desiring revenge threaten a kidnapping.

123. In an effort to show of, one has rushed into great jeopardy.

124. A revolt against authority threatens disaster.

125. One is about to lose his confidence, or have will, or heart broken.

126. Mistaken identity threatens to result in an abduction.

127. One is seriously mistaken for the identity which he has assumed.

128. One whose identity is mistaken is about to suffer fatal consequences.

129. One is about to give way to a wavering or vacillating will.

130. One whose intentions are misunderstood is about to meet disaster.

131. One is about to be severely punished for a justifiable offense.

132. One is about to be compelled to sacrifice honor or principle.

133. One is threatened with starvation.

134. An illicit love affair threatens to cause disaster.

135. One is about to be flogged by a bully.

136. A fatal indiscretion threatens loss of life.

137. One is about to unwittingly break the heart of another.

138. Remorse threatens self destruction.

139. One is about to betray himself to a hypocrite.

140. A disastrous and fatal experiment is about to be tried.

141. One is about to discover the inferiority of a loved one.

142. A trap set for some one else is about to enmesh a loved one.

143. One is about to betray his own inferiority.

144. One is about to fall a prey to the vengeance of a wronged woman.

145. One is about to ruin the career of a loved one.

146. Clever tricksters are about to victimize one.

147. One is about to throw suspicion on a loved one.

148, An infidelity is about to result in a murder.

149. One is about to separate dear ones.

150. One is about to betray himself to an enemy in disguise.

151. A thoughtless act is about to bring disaster to an unfortunate.

152. A loved one is about to learn of one's dishonor.

153. An unfortunate is about to be deprived of a cherished reward.

154. A holdup is in process.

155. One is about to permit a loved one to make a fatal sacrifice for him.

156. An innocent person is about to be led astray.

157. One is about to make an unnecessary sacrifice of his life.

158. One is about to be put "on the spot."

159. Through misunderstanding one is about to overlook a great opportunity.

160. One is being taken "for a ride."

161. Lovers are about to be separated by a misunderstanding.

162. One crime is about to be permitted to cover up another.

163. One is about to betray his secrets to a mechanism.

164. One is about to be involved with an illicit traffic.

165. Disaster is threatened by a boomerang.

166. One is tempted to become a counterfeiter.

167. A great mistake is about to be made because of a dream.

168. A would be thief is about to be outdone by another who is move clever.

169. One is about to desert a loved one rashly.

170. An intoxicated person is about to commit a rash and fatal act.

171. One is about to drive away a loved one by an indiscretion.

172. One is about to place himself at the mercy of murderers.

173. One is about to misjudge or discredit great merit in another.

174. One is about to be caught in an effort to conceal the evidence of a crime.

175. A toe/vivid imagination threatens to bring misfortune.

176. A virtuous woman is about to fall a prey to a designing man.

177. One is about to give up when victory is in sight.

178. A poor man is about to be swindled by "slickers."

179. One is about to be compelled to sacrifice a loved one for another.

180. The knowledge of one's own immoral acts threatens loss of loved ones.

THE CLIMAX

1. Discovery is made that the identity of a character was mistaken.

2. The right of revenge is waived in a spirit of magnanimity.

3. In which the villain does his work so well that it reacts favorably to the hero.

4. In which former associates, double-crossed, wreak revenge.

5. In which the enemy is outwitted or defeated by a ridiculous co incident.

6. A character is unwittingly tricked into a confession.

7. Wherein it develops that a trickster has been tricked or the joke turned on the joker.

8. A lowly character turns out to be an avenger.

9. In which a person discovers that he has been acting under a mad impulse and a change of mind takes place.

10. A woman wronged, unexpectedly wreaks vengeance.

11. Wherein 'a supposedly incompetent witness proves to be a nemesis.

12. An insignificant character proves to be a nemesis.

13. A persecuted character proves to be a kinsman or loved one of another who is only playing a role.

14. A Villain meets the fate he has mapped out for another.

15. In which a supposedly interesting or funny story told by a character exposes his guilt.

16. One character actually helps another by trying to harm him.

17. Wherein a little child is the means of bringing about a reconciliation.

18. An enemy is tricked by friends of his intended victim.

19. In which a predicament acts to save a person from a worse situation.

20. By a prank of fate a villain is thrown in the way of one whom he has wronged.

21. Wherein a practical joke results in a tragedy to an unfortunate.

22. A tyrant is unexpectedly punished by fate in the hands of one who is mentally irresponsible.

23. A misunderstanding of the intentions of another results in an important change of plans.

24. It is prove: that a crime has been committed against an innocent person who has exposed the villain.

25. In which a disassociated accident or incident affords relief.

26. In which an avenger is prevented from punishing his adversary for fear he will be involved.

27. A problem is solved by a. coincidence.

28. It develops that an unexplained act of violence is a delayed vengeance justified by an old relationship or conflict.

29. An unfortunate, expecting ruin, receives a reward instead.

30. A trap set for another enmeshes or threatens misfortune to a loved one of the avenger.

31. A grave danger is finally overcome by the supreme exercise of superhuman self control.

32. Wherein a pursuing enemy proves to be a loved one in disguise.

33. A simple incident is mistaken for dire consequence or ill omen and followed by fatal results.

34. It is discovered that a supposedly absent person is present.

35. The fault of a character, having mused trouble, eventually proves in itself a solution to a problem.

36. Conflict between enemies affords relief to the persecuted.

37. The long-suffering sacrifice of a character is discovered by the person for whom it has been made.

38. A guilty person is allowed to escape because his crime is justified.

39. A person of importance sacrifices pride to right a wrong done by a kinsman or another.

40. A person in jeopardy is saved by an unrecognized one whom he has befriended in the past. '

41. A character assigned to do a wrong does it so well that the effect is just the Opposite from that desired or planned.

42. It develops that an important and dangerous witness is mad or deranged.

43. A secret relationship between persons is unexpectedly discovered.

44. A villain is betrayed by one of his accomplices.

45. A lie having been told by a character complicates matters for him or acts as a boomerang later. '

46. A person discovers that he is persecuting a friend or loved one.

47. It develops that a well-intended act has resulted in tragedy for an other.

48. The use of strategy or where a character feigns to be dead, injured, or vanquished, is employed to save the day.

49. A terrible doom about to befall a character proves to be a role or farce enacted by others for his rescue.

50. An object, which has an important bearing develops to be other than it is thought to be.

51. A spiritual manifestation or sacred memory sways a decision.

52. The discovery that a mistake has been made in the. parentage of a character solves a problem.

53. A character, discovering his own folly, changes his plan of action to rectify it and to prevent fatal results.

54. The apparent appearance of an apparition or occult demonstration saves the day.

55 . A terrible or sudden doom proves to be all a mistake in the identity of a person, thing, situation, design, or intent.

56. Tragic events prove to be only a dream or operation of a disordered mind.

57. An apparently modest and unassuming character turns out to be a daredevil hero and puts to shame those who have criticized.

58. A chain of tragic events proves to be a story some one is telling.

59. A misunderstanding, careless misrepresentation, or failure to act or state the facts, results in tragedy.

60. An apparently tragic situation proves to be a ridiculous mistake.

61. An apparently terrible object of ill omen proves to be a thing of no consequence—a case of mistaken identity.

62. An enemy is enmeshed in a revenge which he has planned for another.

63. In which a character makes a noble sacrifice for another who has a better right. .

64. An enemy is betrayed by. a woman he has scorned.

65. A character, distraught, is prevented from doing a rash act by a simple interference or plea from another.

66. An apparently slain or wounded one proves to be an enemy in disguise.

67. In which it develops that a person has purposely injured himself in order to accomplish an end.

68. What has appeared to be the commission of a crime proves to have been a mistake and that no crime was actually committed.

69. When it develops that a sacrifice made by a character was in vain or too late.

70. The enemy is enmeshed in the toils of the law.

71. In which a mistake has resulted in an unnecessary sacrifice.

72. Disaster is prevented by a strike, revolt, rebellion, or mutiny.

73. The revelation of the unworthiness of a character brings about the discovery of a real love for another.

74. A novel method is employed to delay the enemy until help arrives.

75. A person makes the discovery that he has mistaken his own motions or impulses.

76. An exceedingly clever concealment of a crime is discovered.

77. A character accepts temporary defeat as a means of winning a victory later.

78. What appears to be a fatal situation for a character saves him from worse consequences.

79. The confusion or solution of one problem Supplies the solution of another one.

80. The enemy is confused, demoralized or caused to turn on one another by the clever action of a character.

81. A ridiculous misunderstanding has developed as a result 'of one or both characters mistaking the identity of another or where some other character is mistaken for either or both.

82. The enemy is attacked by his own rivals.

83. An act of the subconscious mind prevents the occurrence of an injustice or tragedy.

84. It develops that a dangerous enemy is only a mad man.

85. It is discovered that a supposedly new affair between a man and woman is in reality one between old lovers.

86. Disaster to person is prevented by a storm or other natural phenomenon.

87. An insignificant but suspicious delay results in the making of a momentous decision.

88. The enemy or persecutor is led into a clever trap.

89. The affections of a character for a child, pet, or memory of an object, place or thing that is dear, brings about a reconciliation or ends a conflict.

90. By temporarily throwing suspicion on a person whom it fits, a character cleverly makes his escape.

91. A character is compelled to make a sacrifice of himself or of another in order to conceal an indiscretion.

92. Retaliation against an enemy brings an unexpected blessing to another. .

93. It is discovered that there was no witness to an act by a character who has thought himself in jeopardy because of it.

94. What is thought to be an enemy or rival is a friend or some other character in disguise.

95. In which a witness whose testimony is feared decides to remain mercifully silent.

96. A character protects or avenges a kinsman or a loved one who is ignorant of the relationship between them.

97. In which a supposedly inferior person solves a problem for a superior.

98. An officer, knowing the justification, takes the law into his own hands and permits a lawbreaker to go.

99. A misunderstanding develops to have been caused by twins or triplets.

100. Escape is effected by the use of a novel means of signaling.

101. The unexpected interference of a stranger whose motives are unknown prevents a misfortune.

102. An unfortunate person is rescued by other enemies of the attacker.

103. In which one discovers that his suspicion of a loved one is unwarranted and was caused by an unfortunate occurrence which warrants sympathy instead.

104. An apparently innocent object or device proves to be a deadly weapon against the enemy.

105. In which a consuming love of the past is shattered by the changed appearance or character of the loved one or where disillusionment and relief from a lover's grief come as a result of a meeting after years have elapsed. (Feet of Clay.) (Shattered Ideal.) (Fallen Idol.)

106. In which a mercenary character is made the victim of his own greed.

107. Where the sacrificing underdog is unexpectedly elevated over his superiors.

108. Wherein a black sheep or disowned child vindicates the honor of his family.

109. Wherein a benevolent character enacts a role, however dangerous, to corroborate representations or a stand made by one who is embarrassed.

110. Where a character who is impersonating another is compelled to be an accessory to avoid detection.

111. The discovery by a character of the blind faith of another in him results in his reformation.

112. A witness whose testimony is feared, is unexpectedly silenced or impeached.

113. Wherein a character whose identity has been mistaken is obliged to play a part and surprisingly makes good.

114. Trusted employee or other character who has refused a bribe and lost great sum thereby, discovers that he has just escaped a trap and is to receive a greater reward.

115. Wherein a character is obliged by his own profession, duty, ,or pledge, to record or seal his own doom.

116. A witness refuses to testify against a person who has committed a justifiable crime.

117. The unexpected appearance of a former inspiring or controlling influence changes threatened defeat to victory—or vice versa.

118. In which a suicide has been merely affected for a purpose.

119. Wherein a clever trickster is tricked by the intended victim.

120. Wherein a prank of fate places a tyrant or other hateful character at the mercy of the oppressed.

121. Wherein it develops that a terrible injustice has been done to a heroic character by overzealous minions of the law.

122. Wherein a character who is suspected develops to be in the service of the law or in a secret service.

123. What appears to have been a lost effort in a certain direction suddenly takes on an important significance in another way.

124. Wherein a character who is about to give way to a criminal or unholy impulse is prevented from entering a life of crime by an apparently trivial interference.

125. Wherein it develops that a person who is under pressure has a greater and more serious obligation than that which is supposed to motivate him.

126. Wherein a plot or crime is detected through the accidental presence of a mechanical witness.

127. Wherein a hard-hearted man discovers that he has been tricked into making a concession by the clever work of a beautiful woman.

128. Wherein the guilty conscience of a person causes him to mistake the identity of a person, object or situation and to indulge in an indiscretion which results fatally.

129. Wherein a mercenary character is so centered on a selfish point that he overlooks a real opportunity which another grasps.

130. Wherein a guilty person misinterprets an accident or mistaken attack as evidence that his guilt is known, and confesses.

131. Wherein a guilty person and the cause of the misfortune of another, discovers that he is making or has made an appeal to his own victim.

132. One who has been captured discovers that he is in the custody of a friend in disguise.

133. A. person who has donned a disguise meets the other whom he is impersonating.

134. Wherein an enemy makes a sacrifice to protect a friend or loved one.

135. Having sacrificed himself a person is suddenly and unexpectedly saved.

136. Wherein a person about to commit murder discovers that there is a gross mistake in the identity of persons or situations.

137. Wherein it develops that a character has sacrificed his life for a loved one.

138. In which a mistake in the identity of a situation causes one to take his own life or attempt to do so.

139. A needless sacrifice is prevented just in time.

140. In which one about to be murdered, kidnapped or seriously injured, resorts to a clever ruse to save himself.

141. In which a mechanical device proves a. nemesis.

142. In which a villain is given a dose of his own medicine.

143. In which a wrong-doer is saved by a loyal servant or friend.

144. In which a conscience-stricken enemy, villain, or rival decides at the last minute to save the one whom he has doomed by sacrificing himself.

145. Wherein one who has evil intentions is outwitted by a clever young woman.

146. In which a clever girl outwits a brutal villain who would murder her lover.

147. In which what was thought to be a dram actually happened.

148. Wherein an unfortunate is saved because his punishment would involve the enemy also.

149. Wherein one is pursued by a friend or loved one and saved.

150. In which an apparently ignorant, unsophisticated or helpless person outwits a. villain or turns the trick on him.

151. In which love triumphs over justified punishment.

152. In which it develops that a villain who is sought for a supposed crime is in fact the hero himself and no crime has been committed.

153. Wherein one is deterred from wrong doing by the knowledge of an example set by another, or by the relation of an experience of another.

154. Wherein a dangerous witness is suddenly destroyed or removed.

155. In which a case of mistaken identity of a person is discovered and a problem solved.

156. In which a case of mistaken identity betrays the enemy.

157. Wherein the discovery of mistaken identity of a thing solves a problem.

158. Wherein the operation of the subconscious mind is a prevention to the commission of a crime.

159. Wherein the discovery of a mistaken identity of a situation solves the problem.

160. Wherein the enemy makes a sacrifice for one who has a better right.

161. In which it develops that an imaginary pursuit of one is only a figment of the imagination.

162. In which a villain or an enemy is caught in a compromising position and compelled to capitulate.

163. Wherein it develops that a supposedly vicious menace is in reality nonexistent, or that an enemy or persecutor does-not exist in fact.

164. Wherein a slight clue proves to be the undoing of a wrongdoer; and absolves an innocent.

165. In which maternal love saves the day.

166. In which the villain or an enemy disguised as an investigator is exposed by the person whom he is pursuing.

167. Wherein the love of a father saves the day.

168. Wherein the brags or boasts of a person results in his apprehension for an offense which has been charged to another.

169. In which a birthmark or other similar means of identification solves a serious problem.

170. In which two villains, both disguised, meet in conflict and an innocent person is absolved.

171. Wherein a fault which a person has, proves to be a salvation.

172. Wherein a blackmailer is shown up in his true light and an innocent person saved.

173. Wherein an unknown benefactor proves to be an unrecognized kinsman or loved one.

174. In which one who is about to destroy himself is saved by the unexpected appearance of a stranger.

175. In which the memory of a person inspires another to do the right thing.

176. In which a vicious animal, reptile or insect proves to be a nemesis to the enemy.

177. Wherein the mistake in the identity of an object terminates in a farce.

178. In which a peculiar characteristic or fault which the character has, proves to be a nemesis.

179. In which cool presence of mind under great stress solves a serious problem or provides a means of escape from a great predicament.

180. In which an enemy falls into a trap which he has set for another.

THE PLOT OF THE SHORT STORY

by Henry Albert Phillips

Misleading Forms of Narrative

THE Modern Short Story is a fragment; yet it is an entity. Details are abhorrent to its very nature. It consists of a few master strokes, and a single figure stalking thru its length and breadth, in the shadow of which every other object and detail pales. Its power lies in the art of suggesting the unlimited panorama of the reader's imagination rather than in the science of photographing the writer's immediate vision. Naturally, then, are we led to suppose that the Modern Short Story is far removed in conception, construction and finish from the following short forms of fiction, which, alas, are often labeled with the name of short story.

We will not attempt to discuss the merits of any story form whatever, per se, excepting the Modem Short Story. Each of these forms that we may take up, admits of artistic treatment as well as the Short Story that will produce perfect gems, of its own class. We shall analyze, compare and contrast them for the purpose of showing what the Modem Short Story is not. And these illustrations are especially applicable, because of the fact that eight stories out of every ten, written by the inexperienced and untutored, belong under these other classifications.

The dictionary honors an "Anecdote with the synonym of " short story." The neophyte in search of training in the art of short-story writing thru the pages of the dictionary, would naturally seize upon this enlightening bit of information and proceed to profit by it But the Anecdote is really the relation of an actual experience of someone, either in the public eye or within the personal ken of the listener, which depends for it§ point upon the humor in the situation, or in the character, or in the manner of the narrator. It is plot-less.

In refutation of the possible charge that this is a Short Story, it is only necessary to say that a Modem Short Story without a plot cannot be. Furthermore, it is not a relation of fact, but the narration of fiction; actual personages must never appear in it, real people must always appear there. Humor may be incidental, but never the point.

Accompanying a large percentage of the manuscripts submitted for publication by novices, is the confidential assurance that every word of their story is true. This is most damaging testimony. Perhaps not one True Story in a hundred thousand is, verbatim, a true Short Story. And at this point, if anyone is kind enough to tell him, the beginner receives his first shock of disillusionment. For the construction of the Modem Short Story is intensely artificial, in the same sense that refined civilization is artificial when applied to a state of barbarism. Truth is so much stranger than fiction that the reading public will not accept it except in the guise of fact.

A True Story then, is the relation of an actual happening or a series of them, that are supposed to bear resemblance to fiction because of their smack of adventure, of the unusual, of the weird or grotesque, of the startling, or of some other qualification that takes it out of the ordinary channels of normal life. But the Modern Short Story does not always aim to present the abnormal. In fact that Short Story is greatest that can present in fiction form the most normal and commonplace happenings in the life of its characters. But it takes artistic treatment to do this. Material must be arranged with a view to effect, there must be a most careful exercise of the faculties of selection and elimination, there must be a plot.

Few need to be told that, while a Fable is fiction, it is not a Short Story. It was one of the earliest forms of shorter narration, and its function was to point a moral. The ancient Fable employed animals as a means to carry its point. The modem Fable, as exemplified in the work of George Ade, endeavors to influence our moral code thru our funny-bone. This form of didactic fiction has not become popular enough to warrant the expenditure of any writer's efforts, no matter how clever he may be in reeling them off, until he has first received a definite order to supply a particular publication with them. In this relation, the Modem Short Story may occasionally resort to personification, but the tale itself must be told unequivocally for the entertainment it gives, and not for the moral it contains.

Another form which has a decided moral tendency, yet which has more than once been successfully subjected to the laws and treatment of the Modem Short Story, is the Allegory. The usual Allegory, with its extended simile without the use of comparative words thru-out the story, depending for its effect purely on its literary merits and affecting the aesthetic sense thru its figurative beauty, rather than the dramatic sense thru its perfect plot construction, is not a Modem Short Story.

Two other forms that are popular among advanced writers as well as beginners, and still are not the Modem Short Story, are the Character Sketch and the Character Study.

The latter may often be made into a Short Story.

The Character Sketch, in the very nature of it, cannot be a Short Story, for the character (hero) must remain perfectly still while he is being sketched by the literary artist In other words, the hero is inactive, while the author is full of action. Of the Modem Short Story the very opposite is true.

The Character Study is too often something in the nature of a surgical operation on the character who is compelled to lie perfectly still while his innermost and vital thoughts and feelings are laid bare with the scalpel of introspection. The Modern Short Story demands either portrayal or delineation of character thru the medium of action, progressive movement, or dialog. And, of course, there must be a plot. One of the most common types, submitted under the label of " short story," is the Humorous Story, While the Modem Short Story may be infused with humor, yet its effect upon the reader must depend once and for all upon the plot, and not upon humorous characters, humorous situations, humorous dialog or dialect, or upon the native humorous talent of the narrator. And, for that matter, we will find that the average Humorous Story degenerates into either a story of Nonsense, or into the Burlesque. In the former, the rule is " anything for a laugh"; in the latter some established, well-known or serious effort is held up to ridicule.

A Playlet is very often written and submitted for editorial consideration under the mistaken idea that it is a Short Story. And it is not necessary that this type of story should be accompanied with stage directions and actors' " business " in order to be called Drama. This untoward result is often produced when an author, sometimes in an honest attempt to write a Modern Short Story, over-refines his product. He seeks after the "unified and tremendous effect" towards which the perfect Short Story aims, and in his zeal loses sight of the fact, that only the Drama may (must) dispense with every least attempt at elaboration. The Drama leaves all, except essential dialog, to other crafts. But the story writer must be his own scene painter, his own electrician and his own stage manager. His story must be played entire on the printed page and visualized in the heart and imagination of the reader. Whatever realism there can be must first be told and thus felt, heard and seen, thru the medium of artistic suggestion. A story written in play form is nothing but a play; and one composed of intense dialog only, denuded of description and introductions, and leaving characters and setting largely to the tender mercies of the reader's more or less prolific imagination, is an unfinished story.

On the contrary, the Dramatic Story is one of the highest forms of the Modem Short Story. But stress is laid, as we shall learn, not upon its dramatic form but on its dramatic situation and effect.

At last we come to the final denomination of a short story, that may or may not be the Modern Short Story, under the classification of Tale, This term has been so loosely used as to almost defy specific definition. " Any fiction story " is a Tale, as far as the present work is concerned. Each new writer of a technical book on story forms helps add to the confusion; one calling that which is contrary to the Modern Short Story a Tale, the other asserting that the Modem Short Story is a Tale. Irving's "Tales of a Traveler" and Kipling's "Tales from the Hills," argue in favor of making the definition cover the multitude of sins as well as the multitude of virtues.

So much for the shorter fiction forms. But the question is asked, again and again: Wherein does the technique of the Short Story differ from that of the Novel?

The Novel aims to present an entire life-career, or that large section of it that depicts and terminates an interesting struggle, or delineates a prolonged evolution of one or more characters thru a series of crises, or chapters. Unity of time, place, person and viewpoint , are observed only in the construction of each | chapter. But the unity of theme alone is demanded of the Novel collectively. One chapter may deal with the doings of the hero, today, in New York, told thru his musings with himself. The next chapter may take up an impersonal relation of the acts of the heroine, a year later, in Constantinople.

The Modem Short Story is, briefly, the depiction of the supreme and climacteric moment in the life-career of its single chief character, cumulatively led up to, and effectively disposed of.

The Novelette is just that—a little Novel. Some writers write very short Novelettes— let us say 10,000 words in length—and mislead themselves into thinking they have written long Short Stories. But the rule of the Modern Short Story applied to the Novelette will soon reveal its points of difference to the student.

The Modern Short Story is a genus — not a species

The Modern Short Story

INASMUCH as we have earnestly endeavored to learn, by comparison, what the Modern Short Story is not, it now behooves us to define comprehensively just what it is. The Modern Short Story is a fiction narrative, short, not merely because it happens to be told in a few words, but by reason of deliberate method employed in its construction. Such a Story must have a well-defined plot / that includes one complete action. It should set out to tell, not the history of an entire life-career, but the story of the supreme moment, or crisis, in a given life, or career. Its chief law is compression. There should be but one great event to record, which should be told as expeditiously as possible, eliminating all superfluous details, avoiding sub-plots. A single impression should be created in the mind of the reader, by having one character take the chief part in the single grand crisis of the story. Every word, every phrase, every incident, should bear direct relationship to the Climax. Economy, unity and compression should govern every element. The story should take place, as nearly as possible, within one period of time; there should be one character to whom all others are subordinated; the one progressive action should, if possible, be confined to one place; above all, there should be one grand Climax, or situation, toward which every element tends with rapid, clean strokes; and, finally, there should be but one tremendous impression left in the mind of the reader at the conclusion of the story.

That is the Modem Short Story, as we should recognize it, before looking into the most important element of technic that enables us to produce it— the plot.

Up to this point, one fact at least must have become self-evident to the reader of these pages: the term " short story " is a misnomer, and accounts for many a misguided effort on the part of those aspiring to write the Modem Short Story. Any short written product whatsoever, that is composed of mingled fact and fancy is to the untutored mind a Short Story.

And, too, a large percentage of our editors need to be educated in the art of the Short Story. At the very least, they should be urged not only to educate themselves in the technical lore of this product that furnishes such a large proportion of their literary provender, but also, to discourage the writers who do not study and practice their chosen art. The public we do not have to worry about Their appreciation is founded, for the most part, upon the aesthetic appeal that any art makes upon them personally, and in this they are certain to be gratified in that most refined, effective and pleasing product in all the field of Literature—the Modem Short Story.

The Plot

THERE are writers who will tell you that when they are ready to write a story, they just sit down and write it. A single character pops up in their minds, like a fairy prince, and bids them follow. Pen in hand, they scratch along after the magic guide, without the faintest idea where the next movement of the pen will bring them—and so on, to the end of the story. This is Romance, in a double sense, that is worth while avoiding.

Suffice it to say, the Modern Short Story admits of no such helter-skelter treatment. There must be a preconceived plot. Furthermore, the short-story writer must, if possible, foreshadow the end of his tale from his first word. How can he carry out this policy at all, if the events to follow even in the next paragraph, are unknown to him?

Not that the writer should disclose the denouement—that would be fatal to his power of holding the reader's interest within his grasp until the end of the story—but, his first word must have a cumulative value, which will be, subconsciously, born in the mind by the reader and shall contribute its share of gratification to him at the end of the story.

You may have an Anecdote, a Sketch, a True Story, or one of the many other short forms of fiction, that may be a gem, beyond criticism, of its kind. But you cannot have a Short Story that has not a plot.

PLOT WIZARD FLASH FICTION - THE PLOT OF THE SHORT STORY

The question arises. What is a plot? And it may be answered by various definitions:

The plot of a story is a cunning scheme devised by the writer, either to make the reader feel the reality of what he tells him, or to gratify his curiosity after having roused it.

The plot of the story is the " working plan " used by the building author. It is the supporting framework, which—after it has been clothed with the beautiful story exterior —is evident to none-except the creator of it. The plot is the penciled canvas necessary before the artist is ready to set about filling in with the color and the scene, the figures and the expression, that make the picture a complete work of art

And yet the plot is something more than a mere outline of the work to be done. For in the plot there must be devised that winding up of suspense or interest that shall later affect the reader with a mental tension that is almost unendurable. Here is laid the plan to excite a curiosity that may be keyed to the breaking point. Preparations are made that these steps may begin with the first word of narration and climb steadily upward, or zigzag exasperatingly backward and forward, until the climax is reached. These are some of the functions of the plot.

The plot is a conscious design, artificial, no matter how you look at it. It is an artifice. But while it is in itself mechanical, yet it must conform to all the laws that shall govern the artistic illusion that is to elaborate it. A story can no more hide a deformed plot, than a hunchback can conceal the crooked vertebrae that hold his life fluid.

Your plot must be just as logical, consistent and plausible as you expect your finished story to be. Therefore, it behooves the writer to thresh out all the difficulties in the way of his progress while he is working over his plot, and not wait until he comes flat against them in the story itself. For this often means that he will have to tear down half, if not all, that he has built, in order to provide consistency and logical reasons for .the change.

The mere narrative plods steadily along, and is interesting only in so far as it entertains or informs the reader. The Short Story must do more. It must elicit his sympathies, prey upon his hopes and fears, and rouse his imagination to a pitch of active service. All this is accomplished by means of

83

the artificial devices employed in the plot, chief among which is the obstacle.

Your perfect plot must have an obstacle.

The chief function of the plot is to create an obstacle.

There must be an obstacle looming between the complete happiness of your hero and your heroine. If you set about to tell the story of their unalloyed happiness, you are merely laying a plan that is likely to bore your reader. He is more interested in how the hero or heroine won or lost their happiness than in knowing to what degree they are enjoying it. Each of the incidents, or minor crises, may consist of an obstacle. The ultimate crisis, or the Climax, of the story, represents the final and greatest obstacle in the whole story, in the process of being removed.

Most geniuses are lawless, and too often suffer because of their talents, instead of benefiting by them

Laws Governing the Plot

ONE of the first requisites of a good short-story plot, is a close observance of the " dramatic unities " of Time, Place and Action. To these the Modem Short Story adds a fourth Unity—that of Person. In this connection, the Short Story and the one-act Play are almost identical in their effort to produce effect. They differ widely, however, in many other respects, since the former relies wholly on the writer to accomplish its purpose; while the latter is greatly assisted by actors.

A plot, therefore, should be carefully designed with a view to preserving unity, or singleness, of effect. And the admonition here concerning the plot, closely corresponds in part to the definition of the Modern Short Story: So plan, or plot, that the action shall transpire, as near as possible, within one period of Time; that the scene shall be confined, as near as possible, to one Place; that the story shall center chiefly around one Person, and that everything in the story shall contribute to one great Situation, or Action, the whole to produce an overpowering, single Impression on the mind of the reader.

The sum of it all, is a painstaking practice of compression. There is a turbulent tendency, when it comes to narrating the story, to digress. To carefully plot, then, is one of the essential elements in the mechanics of the Modem Short Story.

Be careful, however, and see that your economy of details never becomes parsimony. A plot must have every bone that the body of the perfect story is supposed to have.

The problem, and its solution, that confronts the short-story writer, is almost the same as that lying before the architect, except that the writer is artisan as well as artist. If the architect should leave the necessary kitchen out of his plans until the builder should discover the error, and then try to crowd the kitchen in, the perfection of the whole house would be marred. Writers often meet with an analogous catastrophe, in that they fail to provide for some vital contingency of their finished story in their plan, or plot, with the result that they have either to rebuild the entire structure, which is always the better course to pursue, or to follow the course of the house-builder, and make a botched job of it. This is a common experience due to poor plot construction.

The units of the plot are the unembellished units of the story itself. The plot is the potent organism of motives; the story the effective organization of incidents.

The plot of the Modem Short Story must consist of a plan that is as simple as it is concise. It is neither advisable nor necessary to make your short-story plot too complicated. Likewise, a counter, or sub-plot, has no place in the Modern Short Story.

One reason for this rule lies In the need of dispatch, an inviolable Law of the Modem Short Story. Details multiply in the complicated story, and hamper the rapid, clean and

telling strokes that only the simple plot is capable of rendering.

The plot of the Short Story must be complete.

By this is meant that it must comprise one complete action, and not include a complete life, which is the province of the Novel, and might furnish a thousand short-story plots.

As a test of the simplicity of a plot, it should be reducible, in its simplest form, to a few words, or a sentence.

In fine, the method employed in arranging plot matter touches upon the vital characteristics of the Short Story itself. While the plot may be based on real happenings from actual life, those happenings are rearranged according to the artificial requirements of the story in mind. Unessential happenings are eliminated, invented details elaborated.

The plot then ignores facts and caters only to fiction.

Inspiration

WHEN we say that mood should be made a potent factor in the production of artistic fiction, we realize that we lay ourselves open to ridicule from not a few who have succeeded with seemingly no assistance from this mooted quarter. Hard and unremitting labor alone won them laurels. Day in and day out, they dug out their five thousand words, whether they felt like it or not.

> *The anecdotes have it, and they may be true, that the professional humorist has the exterior of an undertaker, and that the sweet girl graduate writes nothing hut tragedy. The one wrote his best joke to pay for flowers for his dead child. The other eats chocolates while she deliberately stabs her heroine to the heart! The artistic value of the "copy," however, of the two scribblers referred to, is apt to be open to serious criticism, for some reason or other.*

Mood refers to a state of mind under the influence of a specific emotion. Mood and inspiration are near relatives. Without inspiration you cannot hope to have an original plot. With what mood you expand the germ of your plot into a logical fiction-plan, that mood is the star under which your story is born and which foretells its destiny.

Harmony of mood and theme is at least courting the smile of the propitious gods; discord between mood and theme, as per examples quoted, is a bid to disaster in treatment.

Some authors, when they have waited in vain for inspiration get in a peevish mood, and deliberately set about to stimulate the desired mood.

They claim that this procedure never fails to kindle their imaginations with lively, original trains of thought.

On the other hand, there are husky writers who will scoff at this "hot-house" method.

Yet, if you will take the trouble to learn what these same writers do, when they arrive at the maddening point where they do not seem to have a single idea that is worth while, where they cannot grind out another line, they too seek their " stimulants" in that form best suited to their temperaments. It may be that they go to a base-ball game, and they return to their work filled with enthusiasm. They too have sought and found the feeder for their creative streak—which happened to be thru a sort of physical exultation—while the other man's is rather thru mental, sensuous or aesthetic stimuli.

Every writer has his healthy inspirational fetish, which it will be worth much for him to discover and to cultivate.

It is needless to say, that stimulants of an injurious nature are not included in this category, even tho Balzac was given to black coffee, DeQuincy to opium and Poe to alcohol.

But, to refer to the experience of actual American writers of to-day, there are those who do get their inspiration from the theater, from the opera, from flowers, from the sight of glorious scenery, from reading poetry—as well as from a thousand other influences that have a peculiar " personal" value.

These authors seek their natural inspirations the moment they get their plot germ; or after a futile struggle with an obstinate plot; or when a plot has yielded a most unsatisfactory story plan; or maybe on all occasions when plotting their story.

Bear one thing in mind. If you are genuinely inspired when you are conceiving your plot, your reader will be inspired to a like degree while unraveling it.

Inspiration by means of " stimulants " then is not " rot," but infectious life.

Mood and inspiration are the heralds of the imagination. And it is only a charity to say, that the aspirant to short-story laurels who does not possess a luxuriant imagination had better abandon further effort in that pursuit. It is not a difficult matter for any writer to test his powers effectually in this direction. The plot requires an elaborate demonstration of the imaginative powers, in fact. With a few bare, telling outlines, the author is called upon to put it all to the test by filling in every detail with his imaginative, or pictorial, sense.

One thing that every writer will learn sooner or later, is that imagination, like the proverbial horse, may be driven to water, but it cannot be made to drink.

The process of plotting requires the most fertile use of the imagination. Writers of experience know too that their imaginative powers are subject to serious variation. The moment those powers begin to grow stale they will not budge. It is time then to switch off. Read an inspiriting book, talk with a congenial companion, listen to a sermon, a lecture, anything that will bring an interchange of thought and get you out of the vicious groove of your own sterility of the moment. Inspire, as we do not need to be told, means to " breathe in." Take it literally, and go seek outside things and thoughts to breathe in. We shall then know the joy of learning that, what Was impossible this morning, proves easy this afternoon.

The Process of Plotting

THE two processes, that of plotting and that of narrating are distinctly different from each other, and should be dealt with separately.

It is the violation of this important rule that accounts for more than half of the failures rejected by editorial offices.

Nine-tenths of all the work done while plotting is accomplished by an exercise of the purely mental faculties. Even inspiration, mood and imagination are called forth to generate new and original ideas for mechanical purposes. The plot is not intended to be a thing of beauty, but an engine of power, strength and purpose. It is the deus ex ma-china. Never once do we let loose our powers of eloquence and elaboration. From first to last it must represent an impassive tower of strength.

In other words, we proceed coldly, artificially, seeking only to convert a given mass of material into units that will best suit our purposes, enforcing our own logical order by twisting Time by the tail, as it were. We deal mainly with facts, or stimulate fancy only for the purpose of creating new " facts" with which to fool the reader. Details, episodes and incidents that have no bearing on the direct line of movement of the story in hand, no matter how much we may cherish them, or how beautiful and effective they may be in themselves, must be ruthlessly thrown aside. We make Selection and Elimination our greatest virtues; and Detail and Digression our greatest vices.

To plot, then, we assume a deliberate, calculating attitude. We view our work dispassionately, soullessly, heartlessly. Enthusiasm we must have, of course, but it must not blind us to our purpose of planning a structure by the aid of rule and compass to be erected within limited boundaries.

On the other hand, narrating the Short Story is a process of fire! With the plot, or plan, in our minds and hearts we commence to build! We give the mental automaton a soul. We breathe life and reality into its powerful frame. We absorb the plot and then, in a way, forget it or suppress it in the flow of our inspiration. We are guided by it, of course. But to restrain our torrent of narration by pausing to think would in a measure be fatal. Narration is a matter of feeling, of emotion, of living the lives and the story within and setting it down without, with a pen, while it is all hot and fresh.

The two processes—plotting and narrating—are as far apart as the Poles.

The same faculties are never called into play, so different are they. It is as if an artist would set out to paint his chef d'oeuvre without measurements, without sketch, without model. But when your mind is engaged with the anxious problem of trying to meet all the stem requirements of the Modern Short Story, it does not stand to reason that it can do its best and most artistic work of telling the story, at the same time.

The necessity to think out plot essentials will not, naturally, keep pace with the desire to tell the story. One is bound to hamper, and hinder the perfect development of the other. The telling part usually gets the best of it, with the result that the finished story often is the story we like it to be, instead of the story it ought to be. It will contain incidents, episodes and details which we cannot ever bring ourselves to sacrifice when we have once created them. The truth is that the plot has been made incidental to the Narration.

If we intend to make the Modern Short Story a permanent quantity in Literature, we must establish working laws conducive to the best possible effort on the part of its writers.

Plot your story entirely, first, before you begin to narrate it.

You will find your work one hundred per cent, easier, and your results infinitely better and nearer the mark of perfection.

Winged Imagination must have some earthly ground from which to take flight, even tho it be the apex of some granite mountain peak thrust into the fleecy clouds of Fantasy!

The Progressive Stages in Plotting

SOME of the most clear-headed and talented writers will have it that they get their plots entire:—inception and conception; idea and motive; hide and hair—out of their own brains with no manner of suggestion from outside agencies. We believe them, of course, because they believe what they say to be true. But is it true? Can it be true? In a small measure, maybe.

Even tho a writer gets his entire plot material from a dream, there must be a whole lot of hard fact mixed up with it. Psychologists tell us that dreams are nothing more than our real experiences carried actively, but subliminally, on by the impetus of our emotions and desires.

> *Take, for instance, the writer who claimed that he was indebted to no outside source whatever for his plot of a Star Maiden who descended to earth and fell in love with a man. He had never read, nor heard tell of, nor seen, nor, in any manner whatsoever, had the ghost of knowledge of a precedent before he set his imagination to work looking for a plot Germ,*

But the plot Germ seldom contains the specific elements that appear in the finished plot. The suggestion for the foregoing plot, wherein the Star Maiden makes her earthly appearance encased in a celestial mantle, was strongly reminiscent of what we might suppose the tail of a comet to be. And when we bear in mind, the recent visit of Halley's Comet, which created the greatest universal emotional impression that has been known for a decade, it is not unlikely that such an idea as the story contained might not have been subconsciously garnered from the store-house of personal impressions, where not among the least of these must have been that created by the sight of that marvelous phenomenon. We might just as readily, think of other concrete, outside objects that might have suggested it.

Bear in mind, then, that tho your imagination may sweep the heavens for a plot Germ, its roots may be always traced to the earth upon which we pass our daily lives.

The plot Germ will not necessarily form the beginning of the story, nor the end, nor the climax. It is merely the beginning of the train of thought that will eventually lead to the complete plot. The plot Germ is usually something striking, that catches our seeking thoughts. It may develop in any direction that will best expand the train of thought that it awakens. It may even be lost sight of altogether, as we inferred in our hypothesis of the plot of the Star Maiden that had been born of a comet.

> *The memory of an old song sung years before, arouses a desire to do again what the writer had done on the memorable occasion when it had originally been sung.*

That was the plot Germ that called forth the plot Skeleton of the following story, that bears little, if any, resemblance:

> *The sad story of the love of two men for one girl, woven round the singing of the old song, "Rosalie," which they all sang together one moonlight night on a road by the lakeside. The narrator, sad because this song is wound around his loss of the girl, the other man, glad because he won her — stole her from his friend. The narrator marries after years, another girl. The other man went to the bad soon after his young bride died. He comes to the home of the narrator and contemplates the crime of robbing his friend. The friend discovers the attempt at the psychological moment and sees but one way to thwart it and save the potential criminal. He seeks a spot from which he may easily be heard — tho concealed — by the criminal, and begins softly to whistle " Rosalie." The night is*

almost identical in every detail with that night of long ago.
The false friend pauses in his fell work, then resumes it. Then
the true friend in his best voice softly sings the song of songs.
At length the other man drops down and weeps. The poignant
memory had split his heart. He quietly leaves the house a new
man.

The first stage in plotting the story is to get hold of the plot Germ.

A host of ideas may come to you with such profusion as to almost capsize
your good intention of sticking to the inexorable rules of the plot of the
perfect Short Story. A single step, however, in the right direction will bring
you face to face with the clear solution of your difficulty. Seek your climax.
This may sound like a singular proceeding. But the reason for it is evident,
when we repeat that the Climax is the point towards which every incident in
the plot is tending with cumulative force. Get a motive for your plot, then,
and every stage in the building of it will be constructed intelligently. Keep
the climax before you as your ultimate goal and you will attain in your story
that singleness of impression and effect that is being harped on continually.

The final stage of plotting the Short Story is the plot Scenario. This consists
of the complete plot preparatory to the beginning of the Narration of the
story. Every particle of the vital motivating matter of the story itself will be
found in the Scenario. Every critical incident and step in the progress of the
story is in its proper sequence; every obstacle is in its place opposing the
progress of the story and spicing it with suspense; until every least problem
has been solved. It stands like an untried, completed locomotive, a figure of
potential power, waiting for the fire to generate the steam that will pour
thru its veins and start it forth with all the grace and majesty of motion and
released energy.

All the writer need do is to glance at his Scenario now and then when in
doubt and then fall to with a spirit of freedom and unhampered inspiration.
If he is a bom writer his hard work is over. There is nothing quite equivalent
to the flow of one's soul fire thru the end of one's pen. That is Art for Art's
sake, which is man's nearest approach to one of the Creator's attributes—
that of making matter out of soul stuff!

BONUS

Who Else Wants to Write Bestsellers That Become Classics?

Get No-Charge Access to
Writing and Publishing Materials
from Our Library Collection

Instant Access - Join Here

Click or type into your browser:

http://livesensical.com/go/writingbooks/

www.ingramcontent.com/pod-product-compliance
Lightning Source LLC
Chambersburg PA
CBHW030009190526
45157CB00014B/1680